Table of Contents

OLDWELL
ANKER
LCOME HOME
REALTY
SOLD
bwelcomehome.com
FLORINE

What Is a Home?

A home is a place where a family lives. One person or many people can live in a home.

City Homes

Cities are crowded. Homes in a city are close together.

Some homes are called town houses.
They are joined together.

My home is an apartment
in the city.
My building rises high
in the sky.

Suburban Homes

Suburbs are not as crowded as cities. Many homes make up a neighborhood.

Some people live
in mobile homes.
A mobile home community
has many mobile homes.

Rural Homes

Rural areas have fewer people than suburbs. Homes in rural areas can be far from other homes.

Farmhouses are
rural homes.
Chickens and goats
roam the yards.

No matter where it is,
each home is different.
The people inside a house
make it a home.

Glossary

apartment—a home that has its own rooms and front door, but which shares outside walls and a roof with other apartments

community—a group of people who live in the same area

mobile home—a small home that can be moved by pulling it behind a big truck

neighborhood—a small area in a town or city where people live

rural—having to do with the countryside or farming

suburb—a town that is close to a city

town house—a home that has its own rooms and front door, but which shares an outside wall with another home

Read More

Adamson, Heather. *Homes in Many Cultures.* Life around the World. Mankato, Minn.: Capstone Press, 2008.

Moore, Max. *Homes around the World.* DK Readers. New York: DK, 2009.

Rotner, Shelley and Amy Goldbas. *Home.* Shelley Rotner's Early Childhood Library. Minneapolis: Millbrook Press, 2011.

Internet Sites

FactHound offers a safe, fun way to find Internet sites related to this book. All of the sites on FactHound have been researched by our staff.

Here's all you do:

Visit *www.facthound.com*

Type in this code: 9781476531182

Index

Word Count: 126
Grade: 1
Early-Intervention Level: 15

Editorial Credits
Shelly Lyons, editor; Juliette Peters, designer; Marcie Spence, media researcher; Eric Manske, production specialist

Photo Credits
Capstone Studios: Karon Dubke, 4, 20; Shutterstock: Atlaspix, 14, eclypse78, 18, Elenamiv, cover (background), FloridaStock, 16, Lindasj22, 1, leungchopan, 10, Rafael Ramirez Lee, 6, Richard Goldberg, 8, Sergey Nivens, cover (front), SnapshotPhotos, 12